Dear Parents and Educators,

Welcome to Penguin Young Readers! As parents and educators, you know that each child develops at his or her own pace—in terms of speech, critical thinking, and, of course, reading. Penguin Young Readers recognizes this fact. As a result, each Penguin Young Readers book is assigned a traditional easy-to-read level (1–4) as well as a Guided Reading Level (A–P). Both of these systems will help you choose the right book for your child. Please refer to the back of each book for specific leveling information. Penguin Young Readers features esteemed authors and illustrators, stories about favorite characters, fascinating nonfiction, and more!

Life in the Gobi Desert

LEVEL **4**

GUIDED READING LEVEL **O**

This book is perfect for a **Fluent Reader** who:
- can read the text quickly with minimal effort;
- has good comprehension skills;
- can self-correct (can recognize when something doesn't sound right); and
- can read aloud smoothly and with expression.

Here are some **activities** you can do during and after reading this book:
- Comprehension: After reading the book, answer the following questions:
  - How many regions does the Gobi Desert have? List the name of each region.
  - How fast can gazelles run?
  - What is industrialization?
- Nonfiction: Nonfiction books deal with facts and events that are real. Talk about the elements of nonfiction. Discuss some of the facts you learned about the Gobi Desert. Then, on a separate sheet of paper, write down facts about your favorite animals from this book.

Remember, sharing the love of reading with a child is the best gift you can give!

—Sarah Fabiny, Editorial Director
  Penguin Young Readers program

*Penguin Young Readers are leveled by independent reviewers applying the standards developed by Irene Fountas and Gay Su Pinnell in *Matching Books to Readers: Using Leveled Books in Guided Reading*, Heinemann, 1999.

For all of the patient, persistent, passionate
scientists and nature photographers
who spend countless hours studying
rare places and animals so we can all
learn more about them—GLC

PENGUIN YOUNG READERS
An Imprint of Penguin Random House LLC

Photo credits: cover: camels: Maxim Petrichuk/Thinkstock, scorpion: marcouliana/Thinkstock;
title page: camel: Iakov Filimonov/Thinkstock, scorpion: marcouliana/Thinkstock; pages 4–5:
Totajla/Thinkstock; page 6: globe: Elenarts/Thinkstock; pages 6, 12, 20, 26, 32, 44, 48: sand:
TeodoraDjordjevic/Thinkstock; page 7: Giovanni Banfi/Thinkstock; page 8: Viktor Glupov/
Thinkstock; page 9: Atosan/Thinkstock; page 10: Fotosearch/SuperStock; page 11: Tian Shan
range: Evgeny D/Thinkstock, Gobi Lakes Valley: Daniel Prudek/Thinkstock, Eastern Desert Steppe:
Wolfgang Kaehler/SuperStock, Alashan Plateau: Tunach/Thinkstock; pages 12–13:
Maxim Petrichuk/Thinkstock; page 14: sabirmallick/Thinkstock; page 15: YKD/Thinkstock; page 16:
NA/Thinkstock; page 17: gnagel/Thinkstock; pages 18–19: Eric Dragesco/Nature Picture Library;
page 19: Xi Zhinong/Getty; page 20: aseppa/Thinkstock; pages 21, 22–23: kjekol/Thinkstock;
page 24: Biosphoto/SuperStock; page 25: JHaviv/Thinkstock; page 26: Colourbox; page 27:
age fotostock/SuperStock; page 28: Farinosa/Thinkstock; page 29: Minden Pictures/SuperStock;
page 30: Yuriy75, CC BY-SA 3.0/Wikimedia Commons; page 31: gnagel/Thinkstock; page 32:
Joel Sartore/Getty; page 33: David & Micha Sheldon/F1 ONLINE/SuperStock; page 34: heckepics/
Thinkstock; page 35: Eric Gevaert/Thinkstock; page 36: Biosphoto/SuperStock; page 37: Oskanov/
Thinkstock; pages 38–39: Tunach/Thinkstock; page 39: Biosphoto/SuperStock; page 40: age
fotostock/SuperStock; page: 41: AOosthuizen/Thinkstock; page 42: Ian Tragen/Thinkstock;
page 43: Eurasian eagle-owl: GlobalP/Thinkstock, jerboa: Juniors/SuperStock; page 44: Xavier Forés/
age fotostock/SuperStock; page 45: agf photo/SuperStock; pages 46–47: Tersina Shieh/Thinkstock.

Adapted from *What's Up in the Gobi Desert* by Ginjer L. Clarke, published in 2016 by
Grosset & Dunlap, an imprint of Penguin Random House LLC. Text copyright © 2018 by Ginjer L. Clarke.
All rights reserved. Published by Penguin Young Readers, an imprint of Penguin Random House LLC,
345 Hudson Street, New York, New York 10014. Manufactured in China.

Library of Congress Cataloging-in-Publication Data is available.

ISBN 9781524784904 (pbk)   10 9 8 7 6 5 4 3 2 1
ISBN 9781524784911 (hc)   10 9 8 7 6 5 4 3 2 1

PENGUIN YOUNG READERS

LEVEL
FLUENT
READER
4

LIFE IN THE GOBI DESERT

by Ginjer L. Clarke

Penguin Young Readers
An Imprint of Penguin Random House

Introduction

Ah-rooo! Do you hear that? A wolf howls in the distance, and another one answers. Look up! Millions of stars fill the cold night sky.

After the sun rises, herds of noisy, stinky camels roam the desert. Smaller animals sleep underground to escape the strong heat.

What is this place? The Gobi Desert! This Asian desert is one of the wildest **habitats** on Earth.

What Is the Gobi Desert?

The country of Mongolia is in the center of Asia, between Russia and China. The Gobi Desert is located in the southern part of Mongolia and the far northern part of China.

The Gobi is the largest desert in Asia and the fifth largest in the world.

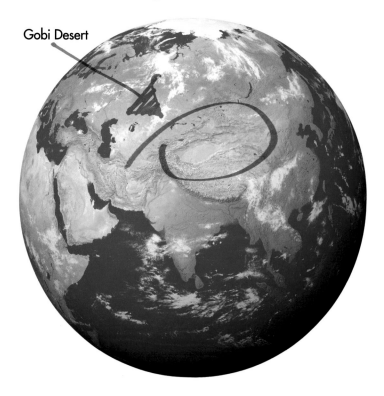

Gobi Desert

The northern part of the Gobi is the farthest place on the planet from a large body of water. The Gobi is quite dry. It gets between two and eight inches of rain per year.

Most deserts are very hot, but the
Gobi can also be very cold. In winter,
the average temperature is -40 degrees
Fahrenheit. In summer, the high
temperature is 120 degrees
Fahrenheit.

It is hard to believe
that anything could live
here. In fact, the Gobi
Desert is the last safe place for many
endangered animals.

The Gobi Desert is divided into five regions, from west to east.

At the far northwest, the Junggar Basin has a few rivers and lakes.

South of that, the
Tian Shan range is
made up of rocky
mountains.

In the center, the
Gobi Lakes Valley
has some sand dunes
and salt marshes.

In the northeast,
the Eastern Desert
Steppe is made of
low, rocky land.

To the south, the
Alashan Plateau is
a high, flat area.

The Junggar Basin

The Junggar Basin (say: ZHUN-gar) is surrounded by mountains. Rivers from these mountains drain into a few lakes in the low, flat basin.

This area is home to the most famous desert animal—the wild two-humped Bactrian camel! It can live for 30 days without food and 10 days without water.

It stores fat in its humps to use when it cannot get food and water.

Slurp! When a Bactrian camel finds water, it drinks 25 gallons at one time! It can even live on water that is saltier than seawater.

Crunch! Munch! The camel eats tough plants with its large, strong teeth. Then it throws up its food and chews it up again. It has terrible, stinky breath.

The camel yells loudly when it is unhappy. And if it is *really* upset, it spits a smelly green slime!

The camel is easily bothered, but the only animal it fears is a gray wolf.

A lone wolf quietly moves closer to a herd of wild camels. *Swish! Swish!* The camels flick their tails when they sense danger. *Charge!* The wolf attacks, but the camels run away.

Some wolves hunt alone, but they usually travel in packs of about five to ten. Working together helps them catch large prey.

The wolf pack's favorite prey is the Mongolian gazelle. But gazelles are very fast and not easy to catch. The wolves stalk closer and form a circle around a herd of gazelles.

Leap! The gazelles jump into the air to confuse the wolves. *Zoom!* Gazelles can run up to 50 miles per hour! Their fast feet fool the wolves.

The Tian Shan Range

The Tian Shan range in China is made up of tall mountains surrounded by the Gobi. Many animals live in this cooler area.

Pallas's pika, named after scientist Peter Simon Pallas, looks like a small, round rabbit.

At sunrise, the pika comes out of its den to look for food. Suddenly, it hears an animal nearby. *Squeak!* The pika jumps behind some rocks to hide.

The pika escapes from a hungry Pallas's cat, but it might not be so lucky next time. This sneaky **nocturnal** cat can climb up and down the craggy rocks to stalk its prey.

A bigger mountain cat is the endangered snow leopard. Scientists believe there are only about 5,000 of these cats left.

A snow leopard perches on a high rock so it can look down the mountain. It spots an ibex below that is away from its herd.

Jump! The leopard leaps down onto the ibex. It sinks its long teeth into

the ibex's neck to kill it right away. This big cat rules the mountains!

The Siberian ibex always has to watch out for snow leopards. This mountain goat is a speedy climber, but sometimes it cannot run away fast enough. Then the ibex fights back with its huge horns.

The ibexes' horns are not just for defending themselves. Male ibexes fight to decide who is in charge. They rear up on their back legs. *Bang!* They leap

forward and lock their horns together.
The fight ends when one of the ibexes
backs off.

The Gobi Lakes Valley

What is the last thing you expect to see in a desert? Fish! But the Mongolian grayling swims in the Gobi valley's freshwater lakes.

The grayling's main enemy is Pallas's fish eagle. This big bird sits on a tree near a lake,

watching for
movement in the
water.

Dive! The fish
eagle grabs a
grayling in its huge
talons. It can even
carry animals larger
than itself!

Like the camel, the long-eared hedgehog can go without food or water for a long time. It hunts aboveground at night. During the day, it rests under rocks to escape the afternoon heat.

The hedgehog's long ears help it to hear a snake nearby. *Grrr!* The hedgehog growls quietly to tell the snake to back off.

If that does not work, the hedgehog rolls up into a tight ball to protect itself. The snake does not want a spiky snack, so it slithers away.

It left the hedgehog alone, but the Gobi pit viper is one of the most dangerous snakes in the desert. Like all vipers, it is highly **venomous**.

The pit viper waits for prey to come close. Suddenly, it shoots out of hiding. *Pow!* It seizes a Chinese scorpion with its fangs and delivers its toxic venom.

That scorpion did not see the snake attack coming. Chinese scorpions are small, but they usually fight back with their deadly stingers—and win.

The Eastern Desert Steppe

The Eastern Desert Steppe is a huge area of dry, flat land covered with grasses and shrubs. The Gobi gecko is well adapted to the desert. Its bulging eyes help it to hunt at night. But it also looks out for predators, like the marbled polecat.

The gecko stands on its tiptoes, opens its mouth, and arches its back. The polecat is not afraid and grabs the gecko. *Pop!* The gecko's tail breaks off! The gecko lives, and its tail will grow back slowly.

The polecat looks like a spotted skunk, and it smells like one, too. The polecat sprays a nasty odor at intruders, so they leave it alone.

The tiny dwarf hamster has lots of predators, so it has to move fast. *Hurry! Scurry!* This hamster's wide, furry feet are perfect for jumping on hot sand.

Hamsters are the main food for the corsac fox. This fox has whiskers on its legs, not just its face, to help find its way in the dark. It also has excellent night vision and keen hearing. This helps it to keep away from predators like wolves and to find prey.

Scritch! Scratch! The fox can even hear a hamster digging underground!

The khulan, a horse-like wild donkey, watches out for wolves, too.

A wolf nears a herd of khulan. *Bark!* The males yell and kick at it. The other khulan scatter and run away. The khulan's only other predator is humans, who hunt them for food.

The saiga, a cross between a goat and an antelope, travels in large herds, too. Also like the khulan, both wolves and humans hunt the saiga.

Snort! The saiga's unusual trunk-like nose helps it to filter out dust in the summer and to keep warm in the winter.

The Alashan Plateau

The Alashan Plateau is mostly flat, grassy plains, but there are surprises, too—the world's largest sand dunes.

The Gobi brown bear is the one type of bear that lives only in the desert. But scientists believe there are only about 25 Gobi bears left. They hope to learn more about this small bear—before it is too late.

Chomp! A Gobi bear snacks on its favorite food, the wild rhubarb plant, in the springtime. This shy bear travels alone and hibernates all winter.

Argali sheep graze in a herd at the edge of the **plateau** (say: plah-TOE). Male argali sheep have huge horns, but they do not use their horns to defend themselves.

Grunt! A sheep warns the herd that he sees a wolf. The sheep all scatter. This does not work very well.

After the wolf kills and eats a sheep, it leaves a mess. That is where vultures come in—to be the cleanup crew.

The bearded vulture eats only bones. *Smash!* The big bird throws a large bone onto a rock to break it open. It is the only animal with this special diet.

The Eurasian eagle-owl sits on a high rock, scanning the desert for prey. It is the largest owl in the world.

The eagle-owl uses its night vision
to spot a tiny Gobi jerboa. *Swoop!* The
eagle-owl zooms down quietly.

But the jerboa has huge ears. It hears
the eagle-owl coming. *Hop!* The jerboa
bounces away on its big back feet. It can
jump 10 feet in a single leap! So it is also
called a kangaroo rat.

The jerboa gets all of its water from
food. It may not drink in its whole life!

Saving the Gobi Desert

The Gobi Desert is most famous for creatures that are **extinct**, or no longer alive—dinosaurs! The Gobi may have more dinosaur fossils than any other place on Earth. The dry desert climate preserves things that get buried especially well.

The Gobi also has many natural resources, such as coal, oil, salt, and **petroleum**. There is hidden treasure in the desert, too! Copper, gems, marble, and gold are mined in Mongolia.

But the Gobi Desert is in trouble.

The Gobi is getting hotter and larger through a process called desertification. This threatens nearby cities. Another problem is industrialization—when a place goes from being wild to being built on and settled by people.

What can *you* do to help the Gobi Desert? If you want to help save the planet, studying science is the first step toward finding answers.

Scientists explore what effects humans are having and how we can undo or shrink these problems. What will you do to make a difference?

Glossary

endangered: animals and places that are at risk of extinction, or dying out forever

extinct: animals that have not been seen in the wild for more than fifty years

habitat: the place where animals, plants, and people are adapted to live

nocturnal: animals that hunt at night and sleep during the day

petroleum: a liquid that is used to create gasoline fuel for cars

plateau: an area of high, level ground

venomous: animals that are capable of injecting poison into their prey through biting or stinging